Case Studies in Managment

The Indian Context

Case Studies in Managment
The Indian Context

Authors

AMIT

MIHIR

NABILA

SHAGUN

VIVEK

MISHA BOOKS
Delhi - 110009

Case Studies in Management: The Indian Context
by Amit / Mihir / Nabila / Shagun / Vivek

ISBN - 978-81-937251-7-7

First Indian Edition

Published by
MISHA BOOKS
2356, 2nd Floor, Hudson Line,
Guru Tegbahadur Nagar, Delhi - 110009
Phone - 9654444181
e-mail : mishabooks2018@gmail.com

Typeset by
Sanya Computers, Delhi

Printed in India at
Sagar Printing Press
Daryaganj, Delhi Delhi - 110002

Price - Rs. 295.00

CONTENTS

SECTION ONE

SECTION TWO

SECTION THREE

SECTION FOUR

SECTION FIVE

PREFACE

The goal of this book is to grab readers attention on how case method help to do problem solving and diagnostic skills for business student, individual and society. If students are encouraged to use their own initiative through groundwork assignments and class discussion, they are better placed to transfer decision–making and problem solving skills into the workplace. Gradually the primary objective of this book is to help the reader 'put theory into practice'. This book is segmented in 5 section according to specialisation of authors, section A is written by Amit Agarwal covering finance related concepts then section B is written by Shagun Tyagi covering concepts related to Finance and Economies, section C is written by Nabila Ansari covering HRM and Management related concepts, section D is written by Mihir Joshi and section E by Vivek Agarwal covering all other concept of Management, cases are ideally suited to business studies, finance, accounting, marketing, economic, bureaucracy in banks, banking and operation management course which offer practical computing skills as an integral part of the course syllabus.

This book is intended for all the management students covering almost every area of management. Each of these cases made with a purpose to enhance the theoretical knowledge of management student and it has its own logic, and an awareness of it can help students to get a practical knowledge to deal with realistic situation and it allow student to think through the question 'why' and 'how' to increase analytical skill.

At the end of each chapter, to test conceptual understanding of the subject and put theory into practice, review questions are included. Throughout the book, simple and easy-to-read style is followed.

We express our gratefulness and thanks to our mentor and guide Prof. Dr. V.K Singh for guiding and sharing his experience and giving constructive suggestions in deciding the structure and content of the book.

Authors

SUMMARY

Alexandre Dumas in his book, 'The Three Musketeers' said "All for one and one for all", making an addition to it, "All for one and one for all, today and even tomorrow". Just what we need to think, when present must be responsible for future. Sustainability comes naturally to the earth but not so naturally to humankind. We are at the brink of time, where resources are at winding up stage. The notion sustainability gives birth to the emotions such as kindness and compassion towards our precious resources; towards the future generation and towards the earth. This penchant phenomenon brings forth the difference between needs and wants. That's how sustainability is related to marketing.

Sustainability is coming to the education in a big way. In global view, The United Nations General Assembly has declared the years 2005 -2015 to be the decade for Education for sustainable development. Sustainability is also introducing in business school.The sheer size of Indian youth is getting paved by education and thus getting more addressed about sustainability and sustainable growth as well. One study reveals that more than 88% of MBA students want to see their future employer actively address sustainability issues. Many universities are designing to start courses on sustainable education for their graduate and undergraduate syllabus.

Modern marketing is the grand child of industrial revolution. Since the beginning of the era of mass production, the practices and philosophies of marketing have evolved on the basis of mass productions with little or no concern with consumer choices and demands. There philosophy was, "if we can build it, we can sell it". In the next generation firms competed with each other through aggressive advertising and sales tactics. The regaining philosophy became let the buyer beware. In marketing 3rd Generation, the needs and wants of consumers took center stage and the marketing concept became the guiding philosophy. The satisfaction of consumer desires was the ultimate justification for any marketing activity. The idea of societal marketing has extended the marketing concept to include concern for social responsibility. This means that while fulfilling the consumer needs, firms need to do so in ways that are not damaging to society. Hence, American Marketing Association (AMA) suggested the new definition of marketing- The activity, set of institutions and process for creating, communicating, delivering and exchanging offerings that have value for customers, clients, partners and society at large.

The old paradigm is broken; we need a new one that is sustainable marketing.So this book throws light upon sustainable marketing. Sustainable marketing is an emerging concept in the world of marketing and business. Sustainable marketing is the marketing practice which emphasizes on meeting the needs of present generation without making the future generation compromise with resources. There are so many issues which need to be addressed by the society. The scope of the book ranges from sustainable product development, pricing strategies for sustainable products, sustainable promotional strategies and green supply chain. The book is distinguished by its extended scope on sustainable process, people's mindset about sustainability and sustainability in physical evidence.

This book tries to make people aware about the sustainable products and their importance. Sustainable products are the products which satisfy the needs of the consumers and that they have no harmful effect on society and environment among whole life cycle as compared to conventional products. Sustainable products include eco-labels, environment free designing, packaging etc. To promote sustainable products companies are making certain policies for their products and government is also intervening in the same way. For many companies pricing a sustainable product is a matter of risk management. Price is an important part of marketing mix. Price is basically a monetary value of a product as agreed upon between buyer and seller. Price and costs are the two different concepts. Costs refer to the sum of money, time and resources associated with a purchase of any product. Pricing is an activity that marketers use to achieve their profit objectives. Pricing depends upon certain factors i.e. demand and supply of a product, cost of production, competitor actions and government policies.

The book tries to explain the concept of sustainable promotion which also forms a very important part of sustainable marketing. The sustainability of the products, manufacturing processes or the firms' CSR activities must be communicated to its stakeholders. Viral marketing, using word-of-mouth (WOM) on platforms of social networking sites aids the brand to aware consumers about its initiative in the field of sustainable development and innovation. Precautions must be taken for greenwashing activities which paves way for consumer skepticism. This book examines how marketing channel becomes more sustainable and contribute to various bottom line goals. The principles of sustainability, member of marketing value networks can enhance business performance and deliver value to customer. This chapter also covers the concept of marketing channel and value network and explores the means of role, relationship and process in the sustainable marketing channels.

Waste is a major factor for increasing cost and problems in marketing channels. Waste is expensive. It costs money to create waste and it costs money to dispose of it. However, if we use the proper waste management techniques, waste can be eliminated or converted into the source of revenue. This topic helps the readers to understand the methods and examples of effective waste management. The Cradle to cradle, closed-loop approach, IWEP (Industrial waste exchange program), IWM (Industrial Waste Minimization), DFE (Design for Environment), DFD (Design for disassembly), overlapping value circles, transparency and chain of custody, etc. are the manufacturing, demanufacturing and remanufacturing techniques to achieve reduction in waste, pollutions and air emission.

Promoting sustainability externally is just one side of the coin. Consumers view brands in terms of the experience they get with the internal people associated with it. Companies should train staff to embrace sustainability not only in practices but also develop an attitude for this global phenomenon. This book also covers the identification of opportunities available in marketing's external environment and their influence on Sustainable marketing strategies. Since external environment is also a part of larger marketing environment, we will also discuss here how they affect each other.

It also unpacks the meaning of physical environment for intangible and tangible products, it is also covers how the physical evidence can be strategically used to best advantage of the consumer employees and the service providers.

Sustainable marketing integrates present with the future. The main focus of marketing is to satisfy diverse needs of consumers, which is a social perspective of a marketer. On the other hand, a business functions for profitability. Sustainable marketing harmonizes the social, economic as well as environmental perspective known as Triple Bottom Line framework of performance. It employs the concept of holistic marketing to blend the 7P's of marketing into sustainability notion. As defined by Fuller, "Sustainable marketing is the process of planning, implementing and controlling the development, price formation and distribution of the product in a way that guarantees adherence to the following three criteria:

(1) Satisfying needs of the consumer

(2) Guaranteeing the achievement of organizational

goals

(3) The process must be in the harmony with the ecosystem.

This book will help activists to understand the footprint of marketing on environment and society at large. It will assist marketing practitioners as well as students in unearthing the integrated sustainable marketing principles and provide a step by step guide in their practical application. It will be packed with relevant examples and case studies. The book highlights socio-environmental priorities, keeping in view the needs of 21st century consumer.

SECTION ONE

CASE - 1

Dispute Settlement Policy for Mr. and Mrs. Malhotra

Mr. and Mrs. Malhotra both run a garment shop, gaining handsome income. They were using the overdraft facility on their current account to its fullest degree. They also had a personal loan from their bank and had borrowed from various private lenders. In Jan 2016, they faces some financial trouble yet uncertain what to do about it, they visited their bank. They discussed their problem to the loaning officer, who disclosed them the bank could give them a consolidation loan to cover all their existing obligations.

Mr. and Mrs. Malhotra were satisfied with this suggestion and they took the loan, which was enough to pay off all their existing obligations and restored their current account into credit balance. Within few months Mr. and Mrs. Malhotra had started to go overdrawn again due to the overdraft facility continued by the bank. In April, having found they were unable to keep within the overdraft limit, Mr. and Mrs. Malhotra visited the bank to discuss the position. The bank's loaning officer arranged another consolidation loan for them, to cover the overdraft obligation.

Again, the bank left the couple's overdraft facility in place, and within a few months Mr. and Mrs. Malhotra were again in financial difficulties. When they visited the bank in November they were given a third credit. This covered the loan that the couple had acquired since taking out the consolidation loan in April. It also covered an additional Rs.500000. The bank agreed to lend them this because they had said they were worried about how they would pay for all the "extras" they would need over the festival time. By mid-2017, understanding that they were not able meet their reimbursement responsibilities, Mr.& Mrs. Malhotra griped to the bank. They said they had requested help in dealing with their obligations however - rather - it had exacerbated things.

Complaint Settled Sasually

Dispute settlement officers considered the bank's underlying offer of a consolidation credit to have been useful, as it re-financed Mr. & Mrs. Malhotra existing obligations into one lower-rate credit. Now, the advance had been reasonable. Not with standing, dispute settlement officers were worried about the bank's reaction when the couple returned in April to discuss their continuing financial troubles. The bank had translated the approach as a demand to get more cash. Be that as it may, as the couple's declaration clarified, what they were truly searching for (and what they thought they were being given) was direction on how be sttoget themselves out of obligation.

Mr. and Mrs. Malhotra thought that taking a further loan must be the best way of tackling the situation, since it had been suggested by the bank. It hadn't jumped out at the couple to look for counsel from any other person on different methods for managing their issue. In our view, the bank ought to have made it much clearer that it was not in a position to advise the couple about their obligations. Under the Banking Code, it ought to likewise have made them aware of associations that could offer obligation counsel.

Dispute settlement officers were especially worried about the bank's activities in giving Mr. & Mrs. Malhotra with an extra credit in November. It ought to have been consummately evident from the bank's knowledge of the couple's income and outgoings that they couldn't manage the reimbursements for this further advance.

Mr. &, Mrs. Malhotra promptly concurred that they should bear some obligation regarding their borrowing. Dispute settlement officers could settle the question by getting the bank's consent to:

- reduce the couple's obligation to its pre-November level
- deduct Rs.250000, in acknowledgment of the trouble and burden caused by its poor reaction to Mr. & Mrs. Malhotra ask for exhortation
- refund any bank charges caused by the strain of November's credit reimbursements and
- Accept reimbursement of Mr. and Mrs. Malhotra outstanding obligation in affordable (interest-free) installments.

Problems

1. How could have Mr. and Mrs. Malhotra avoided the obligations of borrowing in this situation?
2. How is dispute settlement policy effective in managing lending problems?

CASE-2

Issues Related With Personal Loan

A 22-year old under- graduate student, Mr.Rajan worked full-time in a local grocery shop during the vacations. He had a part-time job at the same grocery shop during the normal days. Mr.Rajan applied successfully to his bank for a loan of Rs.25, 000, in order to buy and insure a second-hand motorbike. But when he informed his mother about the loan from bank, she complained to the bank, stating that bank's decision to advance loan to her son had been "*ill-judged and irresponsible*" and that it had taken advantage of her son's ignorance.

Mr.Rajan's mother explained the bank that Mr. Rajan had planned to go U.K for a year after his graduation. She was more concerned that the loan obligations repayments would not only avert him from saving money for his tours, but also leave him in deficiency of money. She also considered that, by lending him the loan, the bank had actively encouraged her son to buy a powerful motorbike in future.

Mr.Rajan's mother argued, the bank should waive the loan and repossessed motorbike in exchange. The bank disagreed, so - with her son's knowledge and agreement – Mr.Rajan's mother brought the dispute to us on his behalf.

Complaint Denied

When the matter was taken to the dispute settlement officers they stated that, it was clear that Mr.Rajan's mother wanted us to take a public position on the issue of lending to young people. We indicated that we couldn't do that, as our part is basically to help settle individual disputes.

When dispute settlement officers investigated the case, they found that the bank had made an appropriate appraisal before consenting loan to Mr. Rajan. They concurred with the bank's view that Mr.Rajan's regular employment and low expenditures implied he could bear the cost of the reimbursements and easily pay off his dues regularly.

Dispute settlement officers did not acknowledge Mr.Rajan's mother's opinion that the lender had exploited her son. He was shrewd young fellow who clearly understood the commitment involved in a loan. Mr.Rajan had already decided to buy the motorbike before he approached the bank and the lender had no duty - or reason - to discourage him. There were no grounds on which they could fairly make the lender waive-off the loan in exchange for the motorbike. Dispute settlement officers rejected the complaint.

Problems

1. What lead to the declaration of the bank loan as ill judged & irresponsible for Mr. Rajan?
2. What steps should be taken to avail such causes in future ?

CASE-3

Analysis of Financial Postions of Mr.Keshav

Mr.Keshav was a youthful, single man with some learning challenges. He lived freely yet depended on his family and his advisor, Mr.Madhav, for help in dealing with his finances. Mr.Keshav had just been in work for a couple of months - as a storekeeper - when the industrial facility that utilized him shut down. He understood there was no genuine probability of finding quick work, so he chose to begin his own business as a jack of all trades. He moved toward his bank and requested an advance with a specific end goal to purchase a van and a few apparatuses.

As his literacy skills were limited, Mr.Keshav had not arranged any sort of strategy for business success. In any case, the loaning officer revealed to him this would not be important and that the computer showed he was "*good for the credit*".. So the bank gave Mr.Keshav Rs. 2, 00,000 as a personal loan.

Excited by the prospect of his new venture, Mr.Keshav went ahead and bought a small second-hand van and some tools.

However, Mr. Keshav was unable to find any job work as a 'jack of all trades'. His current account balance rapidly progressed toward becoming overdrawn and he was not able meet the credit obligations. The bank passed the details of Mr.Keshav to its debt recovery department without giving any prior notice to him.

Extremely alarmed by the tone and content of this letter, Mr.Keshav panicked. Within a few days he had come through to sell his van - at a significant loss –to pay off some of his obligation.

Mr.Keshav at that point asked his advisor, Mr.Madhav, for exhortation. With Mr.Keshav's assent, he grumbled on his sake to the bank, saying it ought not have loaned the money in any case. When the bank denied to accept the complaint, Mr.Madhav referred it to dispute settlement officers.

Complaint Sustained

Dispute settlement officers were satisfied that the Loaning officer was fully aware that Mr.Keshav had only a limited understanding of financial matters. Mr.Keshav had relied on the lending officer and believed that being told he was "*good for the credit*" was an assurance that he could afford the loan. Dispute settlement officers concurred with Mr.Madhav that, in the conditions, it was sensible for Mr.Keshav to have trusted the lender was urging him to take the advance and set up in business.

Mr.Keshav had influenced it to clear when he requested the loan that his income originated from state benefits. He had no reserve funds/savings or different resources for fall back on, and had not been working for enough time to be qualified for any redundancy payment.

While talking about the possibility of the loan, Mr.Keshav had unreservedly admitted to the bank's loaning officer that he had no significant abilities or experience as a jack of all trades - and had not given any idea to how he would obtain work. It was clear that the loaning officer had assembled data about Mr.Keshav's financial position and his purpose behind looking for a credit. But there was nothing to suggest that he had considered how Mr.Keshav would afford the refund. Dispute settlement officers found that it was hard to perceive how any sensible moneylender, looked with similar actualities, would have consented to the loan..

Dispute settlement officers upheld the complaint and told the bank to:

- write-off the remaining loan debt
- refund the charges that had built up on Mr.Keshav's current account because of the failed loan repayments *and*
- Pay Mr.Keshav Rs.50,000 for the distress and inconvenience it had caused him.

Problems

1. What is "good for credit" system that diagnoses the lending process?
2. What caused Mr. Keshav the gradual distress in getting the repayment of loans?

CASE - 4

Personal Loan For Business Ventures

Mr. and Mrs. Negi lived in a town of Kerala. Although neither was in regular employment, they survived on seasonal and part-time jobs.

After seeing a demonstration of a new funfair attraction, they thought they could turn it into a profitable venture. They prepared a business plan and applied to their bank for a business loan, so that they can buy and set up the funfair attraction as soon as possible.

The couple were extremely disappointed when their application got rejected and they asked the bank to review it. Instead their application was again rejected, Mr. and Mrs. Negi asked their branch manager if there was some alternate in which they could get the required loan. Initially, the branch manager told the bank could not help. However, the couple were very keen and branch manager eventually agreed to arrange a personal loan.

Although Mr. and Mrs. Negi ordered the attraction, there was significant long delay before the producers were able to deliver it. So it was at that point part of the way through the mid- year season before the couple could open for business. And still, at the end of the day, they encountered unforeseen difficulties - the town had its wettest summer for quite a long time.

Mr. and Mrs. Negi soon found themselves unable to meet out their obligations due to low profit. When the bank contacted them to repay the loan, they denied and blame the bank. They said it should never have encouraged their project by agreeing to lend them loan. So, they claimed, the bank should be ready to accept a share of the losses.

Complaint Rejected

The bank initially responded to the proposal and made it clear that it did not regard the proposed venture as a particularly good lending risk. So banking ombudsman did not accept that the bank had encouraged the couple to borrow. Mr. and Mrs. Negi had clearly understood that in bank's point of view this was a highly risky business. But they had been insistent that they wanted to go ahead anyway.

Because Mr. and Mrs. Negi had taken out a personal loan, the bank was not a partner in their venture. So, in the same sense that it would not have been entitled to a share of the projected profits, it was not obliged to accept a share of the losses.

Dispute settlement officers rejected the complaint on the ground that the bank was not liable to share their business losses. Moreover officers reminded the bank of its duty to treat cases of financial trouble empathetically and extremely.

Problems

1. Why did the personal loan for business ventures sometimes become unviable?
2. How is dispute in personal loans settled?

CASE-5

Action Against Bad Debts

Mr.Govind, an manager in a cooperative store, applied for a loan from the bank where he had a current account. But within a few months he was finding it a struggle to make the loan repayments.

He complained to the bank, saying it should have made sure he could afford the loan before it agreed to give him the money. He stated, bank should closely observe at the financial transactions of his current account before approving his loan application. And he told that if it had done so, it would rapidly have realised that he had not revealed all of his existing debts on the application form.

Complaint Rejected

Mr.Govind freely admitted that he had not disclosed all his existing debts when asked to do so on the loan application form. Banking ombudsman considered that he was completely fit for understanding both the application procedure and the hazard (on the off chance that he gave mistaken data) of being given an advance that was beyond his means.

Banking ombudsman was satisfied that the bank had not proposed it would construct its choice with respect to any data other than the details provided on the form. It was genuine that the bank could have researched the outgoings on Mr..Govind's current account. In any case, they didn't figure it is reasonable for say that it had an obligation to do as such.

Banking ombudsman dismissed the protestation, however helped the bank to remember its obligation to treat instances of money related trouble thoughtfully and decidedly. Mr.Govind later revealed to them he had drawn nearer a not-profit driven obligation advising office for help with his general monetary circumstance. The bank had consented to co-operate with the organization.

Problems

1. In case of repayment of loans how does the bank take measures?
2. How does the organisation act under the fall in monetary compliances?

CASE - 6

Review of the Account of Customers for Lending

Mr.Frinto filed his complaint to banking ombudsman when he was not able purpose matters with his bank. He had held a current account with a similar bank for various years, and the overdraft facility had dependably been restored consequently, without remark.

So Mr.Frinto said he had been fierce when he found the bank had pulled back the facility without giving him any notice. This had caused him a few troubles, since he had been overdrawn at the time. However he tried to open new account with another bank, in the meanwhile he had been charged considerable interest, at the rate for unapproved overdrafts

Complaint Upheld

The bank said it had made various (recorded) phone calls to Mr.Frinto about the difficulties on his account. Also, it said it could give far reaching inward notes on its concerns about his account, up to the moment that it pulled back the overdraft facility.

During the course of inspection it becomes clear from the bank's statements that Mr.Frinto had been having extensive issues keeping his current account in good condition. However, there was nothing to mention the bank had ever made its worries clear to Mr.Frinto, either among the phone calls or at some other time.

Banking ombudsman acknowledged Mr.Frinto's announcement that the phone calls had comprised of brief demands that he call at the branch for a "review of his account". He had deciphered these solicitations as "standard showcasing calls", made with the expectation of offering him some new product or service, so he had disregarded them. Nothing particular had been said in the calls in regards to his account and he had been given no reason to suspect that his overdraft facility was in danger.

The bank's choice to pull back the overdraft was a genuine exercise of its business judgment. Notwithstanding, we didn't trust this choice had been completed decently. In its view, the bank ought to have given Mr.Frinto a reasonable cautioning about what might happen in the event that he didn't run his account appropriately. Moreover, it ought to have given him a sensible measure of notice before pulling back the overdraft facility.

Also banking ombudsman acknowledged that the bank's inability to give a reasonable cautioning or any notice had caused stress and trouble to Mr.Frinto, since he had been compelled to arrange another account at short notice. So it said the bank should pay him Rs.15000 in acknowledgment of the bother it had caused.

Additionally banking ombudsman thought it unfair of the bank to charge Mr.Frinto interest at its "unapproved" rate, following its withdrawal of the facility. So the bank should reimburse to Mr.Frinto the unreasonable interest it had charged him.

Problems

1. How the credit agency does takes review of the account of customers for lending?
2. How 'show causing' calls are necessary for maintain the lending account balances?

CASE 7

Manisha Restaurant—Delhi

Manisha is a 28-year-old lady and comes from the western part of Delhi. She went to school up to std. VIII and subsequently took a course in home Science. In 1981 she started a tie and dye business after attending a course offered by NGO. She managed to obtain used sewing machines donated through NGO. With the help of two members of her family whom she employed she was able to run a successful business. Demand for tie and dye materials were high and fashionable during the 1980s. With the passage of time, and during the mid-1990s, the machines she was using started to wear down and the material she was producing became out fashioned with the in flow of imported clothes. It was time for her to change to another business.

In 1991 she attended training in catering and with the help of accumulated funds from her previous business and a loan of Rupees 1,50,000 from the Cooperative Bank, she managed to start a restaurant. She used the loan to buy restaurant items like furniture, crockery and utensils and in 1992 she started a small restaurant. She also employed four employees to help her.

The catering business performed very successfully. The clients were mostly common people, often workers in various offices within the Delhi municipality who called at the restaurant for lunch. The restaurant business performed so well with growing demand that it forced Manisha to move to a bigger premise near a sub business centre within the Delhi municipality. She also employed two more waiters to help with the expanded business. Manisha realised that providing service where people were would increase demand for her business. She decided to open two more restaurants, one at the AIIMS and the other near Metro station.

Manisha has paid off the Cooperative Bank loan and her businesses are performing well despite various constraints, such as high taxation, stiff competition from other similar businesses, difficulty in obtaining loans from the banks to expand her business and high price of food items.

Problems

1. What sort of business pattern did Manisha follow to gain Success in a stiff competition environment?
2. Why small scale business like restaurant face difficulties in obtaining loans from banks?

CASE - 8

Kavita Rawat—Poultry Project

Kavita Rawat comes from the Kumaon region and belongs to the rural and poor background. She received education up to XII standard. She served for some time in private sector. She was hardworking, having a zeal to become self-dependent and helping hand to her family.

Kavita Rawat started her poultry project in Jaspur, Uttarakhand in 2001. She managed to build some huts and started business with 100 broilers all funded from her savings. The broiler project was doing well during the initial phase. She needed to expand business by purchasing more equipment and increasing the size of chick stock. In 2004 she applied for a loan from Bank of India and was granted Rupees 500,000. With this loan and profits gained from the broiler project, Kavita Rawat decided to switch over to a layers project. She started with a lot size of 200 layers.

The layers' project performed well and as a result Kavita Rawat was able to repay back the Bank of India loan with interest, even though it took her two years instead of one to do so. The loan was fully paid in 2006. During the mid-2000s Kavita Rawat started to experience stiff competition from other poultry keepers who entered the business. This led to saturation of the market.

Kavita Rawat is now thinking of diversifying to dairy farming where she thinks the competition is not so stiff. She has applied for another loan to fund the dairy project.

Amongst the constraints she has observed with Bank of India is that there is a lot of bureaucracy. Although she had applied for another loan for almost a year now, she has not obtained any feedback.

Problems

1. What steps should Kavita take to sustain her business in dairy farming?
2. How could have Kavita managed to repay her debt to bank?

CASE - 9

Equity Performance: Effects and disclosures

As per the current market conditions of fiscal year 201617 the Indian equity market is performing at above par level. There has been rise in foreign investment allocation. In future the political developments in Europe after the French election, US tax administration reforms and reformations in China will influence the global markets. India is under recovery phase in context to corporate earnings and a confidence in the present government. In 2014 general elections the government formed after landslide victory induced a reason to change the perception of global market towards India. Although we also need to observe the Geo–political events that have strengthen because of easy conversion of stocks or assets to liquid thus improving the growth.

The fiscal year of 2017-18 may receive some unforeseen market behaviour owing to GST implementation. The NIFTYPAT will be driven by the sectors running on cyclical patterns. However the quality of earnings and the bullish behaviour of market possess a risk to investors and therefore it is recommended to beware of the healthy prospects of the market. The reason for such rich evaluation is the liquidity rise in the market where the Sensex is trading near 34000. But there is an enormous fall in real estate sector and simultaneously the huge money flow in the stock market would adversely affect the stock market to reach its equilibrium.

Several factors correspond to the low risk premium such as reform oriented government, Political stability, external account strengthening, Optimum inflation that support the evaluation of premiums. Due to these factors the current market can easily defend the valuations as the number of participants are increasing in the market. In the long term and medium term perspective Indian economy is bullish and focus on bottom up stock Picking. Due to upswing in the world trade positive growth is seen in the Indian exports. The Public sector investments continues to provide support which in turn frees up the blocked capital. Fresh capital investments from the private sector continues to fall short of the requirement. RBI has shown immense hawkishness in the latest monetary policy minutes and believes more improvement in the growth in the FY 18, as current inflation is not sustainable but RBI seems serious to bring inflation towards the 4 % target. Moving Indian inflation sustainably to 4% would require significant productivity improvement and easing the supply side constraints. The government has taken significant steps with regard to manage food inflation.

We expect an expanded respite in the approach rate and the security yields, as RBI is as of now engrossing the liquidity by means of switch repo sell-offs and Issuance of MMS securities. Additionally from the more drawn out term point of view security yield are comprehensively positive, guided by diminished hazard premium for Indian G-secs, desires of polity continuity and reform momentum in the nation.

The change in India's financial essentials, authoritative and administrative change, dis intermediation of the credit advertise – all sets down positive accounts for the loaning market.

Problems

1. How does inflation affect the equity investors due to rate cuts and rises in interest rates by RBI?
2. How do the geo-political event influence the Sensex market? Elaborate.

CASE - 10

K.M. Joshi Hardware Store-Haldwani

Mr. Joshi started business in Haldwani town in 1998 with a retail grocery items shop selling a variety of food items. Hemoved into self-employment after completing senior secondary school education. After making a reasonable amount of profit, in 2002 he decided to move into the hardware business. Hardware business in Haldwani town had for a long time been a monopoly of U.P and Delhi traders and was seen to begene rating good profit.

Business Performance

The hardware business started to expand as more and more profit was made. He also employed his wife as an assistant manager and had one shopkeeper. Demand for hardware items has been expanding rapidly in many parts of Uttarakhand mainly because of the expanding construction of the real estate projects and industry following the economic reforms of the Uttarakhand Government.

Mr. Joshi took advantage of this expansion in demand for hardware items and planned to expand his business. In 2003 he applied for a loan from Uttarakhand Gramin Bank and was granted Rupees 12,60,000. He used his loan together with profits generated from his business to expand his stock and added other types of building materials. He also moved his business to a larger premise, which could accommodate the expanded stock. Increase in price of building materials and stiff competition, has forced him to give credit to some of his good customers, which is having a negative effect on his business. Mr. Joshi procures most of his materials from Orrisa state, far away from his place. The cost of hiring transport has also risen, and is affecting the business negatively.

Discussion and Evaluation

Mr. Joshi reported making 'very' good profit. Through profit generated from this business he has been able to repay the Uttarakhand Gramin Bank loan with interest (a total of Rupees 14,30,000). He has also been able to build a modern family house. Through income from the business he has been able to pay school fees for his two children attending private secondary schools.

It is the existence of opportunity and Mr. Joshi's business skills more than any thing else that have contributed to his success. Also the credit from Uttarakhand Gramin Bank facilitated the expansion of his business. Without the loan at the material time, this expansion would have taken longer to achieve.

Problems

1. How Mr. Joshi procured the material from a faroff place from his residence at a cost that he was able to cover his loan?
2. Was it Mr. Joshi's business skills that gave him success or the rising demand for infrastructure materials.

SECTION ONE

Mihir Joshi

CASE - 1

Sanyog Fabricators Pvt. Ltd.

Kamal is mechanical engineer from IIT kharagpur and is a promising entrepreneur. His father owned a small scale business unit for the manufacturing of electrical switch boards. His father's business unit, *Sanyog and sons* was mainly catering the requirements of local builders, local dealers and retailers. Kamal took over the company's lead in hand few years ago and relieved his father. After 3 years of understanding the trade and policies related to trade, Kamal decided to expand the business and become a large scale business holder.

He established a Pvt Ltd. Company and renamed the enterprise to *Sanyog Fabricators Pvt. Ltd.* And included his two brother and close friends as directors and Senior Associates. The investment for the firm was decided to be done by the directors and few angel investors. Mr. Kamal's project started with great expectations and things went linearly. He did not face any issues related to finance as the net capital and availability of assets was good. *Sanyog Fabricators Pvt. Ltd.* started gaining market and developed goodwill among customers with high quality products and services. The company became a leading supplier and producer of high quality electrical switch boards, capacitors and other electrical equipment. The capacity of production was 15 tonnes per month. The order position was also more than 12 tonnes per month and

Mr. Kamal was getting new customers to cover the complete 15 tonnes per month in coming months. The demand in the market for *Sanyog Fabricators Pvt. Ltd.* rose to an unbelievable position. Within year of Production Mr. Kamal had to increase the plant capacity to 25 tonnes per month.

The Technical Issue

Of all the machinery available power press is the most important machine that could produce 35 tonnes of pressed components per month. The other fabrication machines like drilling, nibbling and smoothening have been at only par level but not above that. Three of the customers have asked for a regular demand and are going to enter into a legal contract for 20 tonnes per month. There are also some signs in increase of the number of customers in far off areas and the trend shows an increase in the next two quarters. In order to cope up with the situation Mr. Kamal decided to increase the production capacity of the plant. He doubled the production capacity of drilling, welding, punching, and nibbling machines.

A high investment is required for coating material and coating process and so he added only one extra machine for this purpose. Mr. Kamal was very happy and optimistic with the increasing demand. However, the issues of low production capacity machine made him think twice before accepting any new orders. His floor manager suggested him to out source the work to other companies and accept all the orders. Mr. Kamal being highly conscious about the product quality was not ready to accept all the orders as any time lag may dent his company's image.

Problem

1. How should Mr. Kamal deal with the ever increasing demand of his company products?
2. What type of production plan should Mr. Kamal take in order to secure the quality and goodwill of his company?
3. Discuss if you being the floor manager at Sanyog Fabricators Pvt. Ltd what would you suggest Mr. Kamal in taking up or not taking the new order flows.

CASE - 2

Clean Edge

Clean Edge is a bleaching company that processes Nylon fabric for an MNC. The company production facility produces Nylon fabric at 100 metres per hour. The unit is supposed to make a lot of pollution but the activity is to remain under the supervision of PCB or the Pollution and Control Board. The units cannot go for the production unless they receive the letter of consent from the board. The company has two effluent management plants. The board gave them permission to set up their own effluent management plants on yearly inspection basis.

The plant for managing the waste has a capacity to handle 100 litres per minute and is highly efficient. The company received the grant from Fin Corporation for setting up the plant. However, in the mid-way of the erection plant the company faced issues concerning the discharge of the waste as the area in which the waste had to be discharged belongs to the National Highways authority.

The company has to receive the consent from the Highways authority as the discharged effluent made a peculiar vapor that might create allergies. Another issue that the company faces is that the units that had to merge with the firm have backed down from merging with the company. The company faces two major issues in setting up the effluent discharge plant and simultaneously, the final project.

Problem

1. Discuss the project and the issues associated with it.
2. What steps should the company follow to get the project running?
3. Should the company transfer the effluent plant setting up rights to the PCB?

CASE - 3

Sherman: The Entrepreneur

Sherman started a small company based on medicine research and development. Sherman started the business in early 2000's and gained a lot of market. He introduced new hair oil in the market that can help bald people get their hairs back. Sherman used a functional organization design in due process. The hair oil market had several brands that posed a definitive challenge for Sherman's firm but none of them claimed that they can give hope to people hair loss issues.

Way to Italy

The tests in the laboratories were highly successful and paved the way for Sherman to set up the company in Italy. The Italian firm asked Sherman to produce 1000 litres of oil every month and in return they will manage the marketing and sales for Sherman in Italy and European market. Sherman was very positive and so enthusiastic on working with the Italians that he took up the order without analyzing the challenges.

Sherman started reaching the break even limit of the Indian market but lagged in the Italian market due to issues related to the production facilities. The Italian firm that managed the marketing for Sherman's company started losing the market due to the product quality related issues. The hair oil needed some items that were supplied only from India but in quest to increase the production Sherman decided to find the material in Alps. But the material from Alps didn't have that much quantity level that Indian firm offered but Sherman decided to go with the product.

The production quantity decreased and Sherman started losing the market after the material supply. In one year of the firm's establishment the Italian unit had to be shut down and Sherman faced heavy losses. In order to pay his debt Sherman had to sale half of his Indian business however, some new products were still there to Sherman's rescue. The material for these products was supplied from Nepal and the Nepalese company asked Sherman to set up the firm in Nepal where the production cost is very less. Sherman having faced a bitter taste of Italian market faces a dilemma.

Problem

1. What went wrong for Sherman in Italy? How it should have been managed?
2. Do you think every entrepreneur should avoid risk?
3. What shall be Sherman's decision for Nepal?

CASE - 4

Single Piece

Single Piece is a new garment showroom in the city of

Pune where there are a large number of shopping malls, stores, brand retailers and dealers. The Single Piece owner Samayra is an interior designer and an MBA. She also holds a doctorate degree in management but instead of making her career in academics she decided to start her garment showroom in the North of the city along with her brother. Single piece offers a wide range of women clothing like Designer sarees of well-known designers like Satyapaul, Lehengas from Ludhiana, Designer Suits and wedding gowns.

Her brother is a fashion designer and wants to start his own cloth lining in future. Single piece has been designed in a very creative way like fall ceiling is in shape of vaulted pediments that gives it an exceptional look. The dress material starts from Rs. 5000 and goes uptoRs. 100,000. The sales of the first month have been high but little less than the expected. However, Samayra is very hopeful to achieve the expected target in first six months.

The consumers after the purchasing from the store were very thrilled to see the interior designs of the store. They complemented Samayra and his brother for this wonderful effort. Although few customers are not happy with the prices offered by Single Piece. They demanded for offers and discount which Samayra could not afford to give in the initial month. Some customers even said that they were getting same material at a lesser cost and at a renowned brand. Samayra was also facing publicity issue because of their location. The location of the store was near to the central market but there were several brands also in the same lane. This was an uphill task for

Samayra to help Single Piece take a successful flight. In order to promote Single Piece Samayra's brother set up one LED over the top of a highest tower at a staggering cost. He also engaged one advertising firm for this purpose. For Samayra the big challenge is to maintain investment cost as she took 20 lacs loan from a Cooperative bank.

Problem

1. As an advertising firm what steps should you take?
2. How should Samayra manage the investments? Devise an investment plan.
3. Is the promotion step taken by Samayra's brother correct? Comment.
4. Will the performance of single piece improve after the advertising plan has put into action? Discuss

CASE - 5

A company with no Venture Capital Financing

Abby and Ray both have software engineering backgrounds and experience working on venture-backed start-ups. In past Abby founded Truder, a Web site that allows users to create interactive maps. Ray is the former chief technology officer of an information technology company. The two founded Viscosity with the shared goal of building an agile company providing security services.

From the beginning, the founders were determined to try bootstrapping. Abby said she may have taken help from Venture capitals but no one came with a nice offer. Though their relationship has been good with the investors still people had doubts to their plan. Ray thought same that why to take money from outside investors when it can be built on without VC funding. Viscosity has stuck with its plan to bootstrap, releasing a series of experimental products with the hope that at least one will catch on and begin generating the revenue needed to build the company. They launched prototypes of models that would help them gain some capital from the market, even sell them so as to get their firm on ground.

One of the products is Secret Sharer where anyone can share their thoughts feelings, deepest desires, crushes and even form anonymous office groups to talk about bosses. The product has gained many users 1000 in a month and both Abby and Ray are positive. They soon will launch an android app that will help them gain wider access to the customers. Though, it is too early to tell whether users are achieving their objectives. The partners have ideas for 10 to 20 more products, but have concluded that they must focus on their current offerings until they succeed - or fail. They recognize that if multiple products show promise simultaneously, they will not have the resources to achieve them all. Also it might not be possible to handle so many applications without minimum of 20 employees that they cannot afford. It is risky say the existing competitors of the market. They believe bootstrapping the resources might be tough call to start a business in surprisingly shrinking market benefits.

Problem

1. What should be Abby and Ray's decision?
2. Does the VC capital hinders the founders ability to increase number of applications?

CASE - 6

Micro Customers Big Profits

Roger and Samuels started a tea packaging company at a time when whole world was afraid of losing bank accounts. They had a great arrangement to take on the coffee market which is very popular in Smallville. While Roger knew how to interact with customers, Samuels knew how to get the investors on board. They started Big T with 1 million dollar of investment.

At first, Roger and his partner agreed on strategy. With their industry contacts, they said they believed they could land accounts from major bands. Focusing on high volume orders made sense to them in part because Big T suppliers offered a price break on large quantity orders. But the partners did not realize that most bands were locked in to long-term contracts. His partner continued to believe big orders were highly necessary to generate large chunk of profits and neglected the small orders. Besides he was hopeful that he would win the key accounts by nice office presentations. This started creating a rift between the partners. After a year of business Roger bought out his partner's share but the market crashed heavily. At that point, he decided that no order was too small. He would find a way to take all business. Once he made a decision to take all orders, Rogers reassessed his costs and determined that he could make a profit on the smaller orders. He even reduced the prices of the tea packets. So Big T survived the market crash that Roger believes is a lesson that no customer is small and every individual is important.

Problem

1. Is long term strategy a better option when the market is vulnerable?
2. What could possibly a new entrant's strategy to set a course of business?

CASE - 7

A Cosmetic Label

As a purchasing manager for a large Asian cosmetic firm, it is important to know about all the ingredients needed to make a fairness cream. The label for the firm is as important as the product quality. However, many firms have entered the market with their own labels and have increased their product mix in the market. The company is looking to facelift their brand with more products and better graphics.

The existing supplier for the firm has supplied the firm with raw material for over twelve years and one third of the business is accounted for the supplier by the firm. The relationship of the purchase manager is very nice with the accounts manager of the supplier but the company is moving forward with rigorous advertisement policies for which they need more money. A new competitor of the supplier is offering products at 10% discount that would save the firm more than two quarters of initial investment. The products offered are state of the art and do not require animal testing. However, the old supplier is also offering a concession of 4% on all the products in addition to the new chemicals still to be launched in the market.

Problem

1. What are the ethical issues in this business deal?
2. How would you as a purchasing manager proceed in such situation?

CASE - 8

A Good Saleswoman

Collin, 29, has recently been promoted to manager of sales personnel at a large motorbike dealership. Simmy, a new salesperson (and the only female salesperson), comes to his office late one afternoon with a complaint about something she says really bothers her. Specifically, she says she has never seen Tom, one of the most experienced (and best) salespeople, at any of a series of off-site training seminars (at which attendance is supposedly required). These seminars are designed to help sales staff learn detailed technical information about the mechanical advantages of the cars they sell.

Collin's "grapevine" impression is that most salespeople think the training seminars are a joke, and rumor has it that a lot of salespeople regularly skip them (although many salespeople can be heard saying things like, "I'm out of here-I'm going to today's seminar at the Hyatt"). Collins' boss, however, regularly sends him memos that stress the importance of the training. Upper management spends a lot of money on the training seminars, because they feel that such training will give the dealership a competitive edge. Simmy is so new that she does not yet have an established sales record. Also, Collin has heard through the grapevine that a lot of the salesmen are uncomfortable with Simmy and wonder if a female can learn to sell motorbikes. She seems eager, however, and obviously wants to follow the rules. She concludes by telling Collin that she'll check back with him tomorrow to see how he's handling the issue of the absent salesman.

Problem

1. What should be the decision of Collin?
2. How can Simmy change her perception around?

SECTION THREE

Nabila

CASE - 1

SAS Institute Invests in Employees

SAS is one of the world's largest privately held software company. They have over 20000 employees worldwide, operate in over 150 countries. The company is quick to attribute their success to the performance and loyalty of their workforce. This is directly correlated with how they treat their employees. SAS has perfected the art of employee management. Employees seem to genuinely enjoy working at SAS and are unusually attached to the company, resulting in less a turnover rate.

One thing SAS does well is giving its employees opportunities to work on interesting and challenging projects. The software developers have the opportunity to develop cutting-edge software to be used around the world. The company makes an effort to concentrate its business in the areas of analytics, which add the most value and help organizations best analyze disparate data for decision making, creating opportunities for SAS workers to be challenged. Plus, the company removes obstacles for employees. Equipment, policies, rules, and meetings that could impede productivity are eliminated. One of the best supports of SAS to its employee is that it has treated employees well in bad times as well as in good times. Too many companies worldwide sacrificed employees and benefits to cut costs in 2009. SAS took the opposite stance, and we have been rewarded in employee loyalty and overall success of the business.

Maintaining this position throughout the downturn puts us in the best position to meet the expected market upturn."

Problem

1. What differentiates the SAS employee management with that of other companies?
2. How does an employee contemplate the idea loyalty in presence of global competition?

CASE - 2

A Motivating Place to Work: The Case of Ziba

Ziba is one of the well known company selling product online is known for its 365-day return policy and free shipping as it is for its innovative corporate culture. Ziba being popular among youngster to work for because of its motivation ability, and the working environment. Ziba seems to be creating an environment that encourages motivation and builds flavour. The company delivers above and beyond basic workplace needs and addresses the self-actualization needs that most individuals desire from their work experience. Company believes that the secret to customer loyalty is to make a corporate culture of caring a priority. During the interview process, applicants are asked questions relating to the company's values, such as gauging their own weirdness, open mindedness, and sense of family. For example, there is no limit to the time customer service representatives spend on a phone call, and they are encouraged to make personal connections with the individuals on the other end rather than try to get rid of them.

Although Ziba has over 1,300 employees, the company has been able to maintain a relatively flat organizational structure and prides itself on its extreme transparency. In an exceptionally detailed and lengthy letter to employees, top level managers of Ziba spelled out what the new partnership with another similar firm what would change, and more important, what would remain the same. As a result of this type of company structure, individuals have more freedom, which can lead to greater satisfaction. Although Ziba pays its employees well and offers attractive benefits such as employees receiving full health-care coverage and a compressed workweek, the desire to work at Ziba seems to go beyond that.

Problem

1. What potential organizational changes might result from the acquisition by Amazon?
2. Why do you think Ziba' approach is not utilized more often? In other words, what are the challenges to these techniques?

CASE - 3

Effect of Global Economic Downturn

Suppose ABC is a central university, based in the south of India, and has gained an excellent reputation for its postgraduate courses. As a result, in recent years the University has attracted a large number of international postgraduate students. However, this year there has been a noticeable reduction in the number of applications from international students. The University authorities are unsure if this is because of the global economic downturn, or if there are other factors causing this reduction. They have decided to conduct research to investigate how studying at Central University is now perceived by potential students and by key groups of opinion formers, such as education bodies and major employers.

Problem

1. According to you what has been a noticeable reduction in the number of applications from international students?
2. Design a marketing research plan for them?

CASE - 4

Success of (MkIS). The Case of SMEs

This case study deals with synthesis of the survey based results for 140 SMEs from the three sectors, i.e., cutting tools, sports goods and bicycle components from Punjab, India and also analysis for six firms of which two firms producing Cutting Tools, two firms producing Sports Goods and two firms producing Bicycle Components, respectively. The synthesis is done keeping success factor of Marketing Information System (MkIS) as a dependent variable of the MkIS Model. The independent variables of the study are: MkIS Design Characteristics, Capabilities of MkIS, Primary Characteristics of MkIS,

Hindrance Factors of MkIS and Factors underlying MkIS Sophistication. It is analysed that Accurate Information and Timely Information are the top priorities amongst the MkIS Design Characteristics. High priority is given to sophisticated analysis of data with an ability to make recommendations as an aid to decision-making and provides valuable decision support information as the top priorities amongst the Capabilities of MkIS. It is analysed that e-mails along with processed information maintained in the database are the top priorities amongst the Primary Characteristics of MkIS.

Further, the belief is that the computerized MkIS can solve all the management problems of planning and control of the business as well as MkIS is conceived as a data processing system and not as an information processing system in the database, which are the top priorities amongst the Hindrance Factors of MkIS. Also, it is analysed that meeting customer needs and threat to new entrants are the top priorities amongst the Factors underlying MkIS Sophistication in the Survey-based Results and Case Study Analysis respectively. At the end, framework of MkIS Model is taken with top two factors of each independent variable of MkIS in three categories namely, cutting tools, sports goods and bicycle components with the analysis of synthesis of the survey based results of 140 SMEs and case study respectively for highlighting the overall scenario of Success of MkIS Model.

Problem

1. Examine the critical factors for the development of MkIS Model for the selected manufacturing SMEs of Punjab.
2. Develop a framework of MkIS Model for selected SMEs of Punjab.

CASE - 5

Promotional Tools for BAS

Building Audits (BAS) is a partnership company established in 2001 by two young entrepreneurs, Mr. Kale and Mr. Gokhale, for providing quality audit services in Pune. With a market survey BAS found out that people appreciate such type of rating system. But the main hitch was absence of similar product in the market. So, the success of the product was dependent on the promotion strategy implemented by the company. There was a difference of opinion amongst the partners on the promotional strategy. Mr. Gokhale was of the opinion that BAS should only focus on the builders, where as Mr. Kale was of the opinion that they should also target the flat owner's. So, both of them gave this key task of developing the promotional strategy to their young, energetic marketing manager, Akash. Akash was contemplating on all the options suggested to him for promotional strategy and was thinking which one to be presented on the D-day.

Problem

1. Discuss various promotional tools available in B2B markets.
2. To assist students in designing a step-by-step promotion strategy development process.

CASE - 6

Cereal as a New Entremets Market

A major cereal manufacturer produces and markets standardized breakfast cereals to countries around the world. Minor modifications in attributes such as sweetness of the product are made to cater to local needs.

However, the core products and brands are standardized.

The company entered the Chinese market a few years back and was extremely satisfied with the results. The company's sales continue to grow at a rate around 50 percent a year in China and other Asian countries, and based on the market reforms taking place, the company started operations in India by manufacturing and marketing its products. Initial response to the product was extremely encouraging, and within one year the company was thinking in terms of rapidly expanding its production capacity. However, after a year, sales tapered off and started to fall. Detailed consumer research seemed to suggest that while the upper-middle social class, especially families where both spouses were working to whom this product was targeted adopted the cereals as an alternative meal (i.e., breakfast) for a short time, they eventually returned to the traditional Indian breakfast.

The CEOs of some other firms in the food industry in India are quoted as saying that non-Indian snack products and restaurant business are the areas where MNCs can hope for success. Trying to replace a full meal with a non-Indian product has less of a chance of succeeding. You are a senior executive in the international divisions of this food MNC having postgraduate qualification in management from IGNOU and several years of experience of operating in various countries in a product management function. You have been appointed head of the fact finding mission to determine answers to these specific questions. What, in your opinion, would be answers to these questions?

Problem

1. Was entering the Indian market with a standardized product a mistake? Justify.
2. Given the advantages to be gained through leveraging of brand equity and product knowledge on a global basis, and the disadvantages of differing local tastes, what would be your strategy for entering new markets?

CASE - 7

Impact of Business Environment on Business Performance

KFC, a fast - food operator, faced immense resistance from some politically active consumer groups when it opened its operations in India. One group proclaimed that opening KFC outlets in the country would propagate a "junk-food" culture. Others proclaimed that this way " the return of imperialistic powers" and was an attempt to "Westernize the eating habits" of Indians Overzealous local authorities in the city of Bangalore used a city law restricting the use of MSG (a food additive used in he chicken served by KFC) over a certain amount as a pretext for temporarily closing down the outlet, despite the fact that the authorities did not even have the equipment to measure the MSG content in the proportions stated in law. In the capacity city of New Delhi a KFC outlet was temporarily closed down because the food inspector found a "house-fly" in the restaurant. Both of these issues got resolved through hectic consultations with these consumer groups and through legal orders issued protecting the interests of the outlets.

Problem

1. In view of the above situation, critically examine the impact of social and political environment on a firm's operation in international markers.
2. After completion of your MBA from IGNOU, suppose you have been appointed Country Manager (Indian Operations) in KFC, what steps would you take to cope up with the situation?

CASE - 8

BMW: Marketing Subsidiaries in Foreign Markets

BMW is a German manufacturer of high-quality motor cars; about half of its sales are in the German market, with the other half from exports. In reappraising its markets and distribution strategy both in Germany and abroad, the company believed that its multiple layers of distribution were causing inefficiencies in its marketing efforts.

BMW Germany

Originally, BMW had a dual distribution system in Germany. It employed a strong wholesaler system along with direct distribution by BMW to large dealers. This system seemed to work effectively because BMW's market share in Germany doubled in 10 years. However, the company found share competitive distortions with this dual approach. For example, the wholesalers that received the same commission for wholesale transactions as for retails sales had gone into direct competition with retailers. The larger direct dealers sometimes sold more than the wholesalers but received the smaller dealer discount. The problems arising from BMW's distribution strategy caused the company to abolish its German wholesaler network. BMW expanded its direct dealer system to replace the business formerly handled by the wholesalers.

BMW Abroad

The company was planning to initiate a more direct selling method in its foreign markets as well as at home. It realized the need for care in order not to disturb existing import channels. However, the company believed that it was desirable to replace the present independent importers in foreign markets with company-owned marketing subsidiaries. The independent importers buy the cars from Germany and then resell to accredited dealers - who sell them to the public, In moving to company-owned marketing subsidiaries, BMW was following the international marketing approach of

Volkswagen and Daimler-Benz (with Mercedes). One of the major arguments presented for going direct was that BMW could save the 15 percent commission the company paid to its importer distributors in foreign markets.

France

In line with its new policy of more direct distribution in foreign markets, BMW formed its first marketing subsidiary in France. BMW Import SA replaced the former independent French importer (which had been called BMW France but now was renamed SFAM France). SFAM France continued to sell BMW cars to consumers through its retails outlets in Paris and in the provinces. Sales to dealers henceforth were made only by BMW Import SA, the company's wholly owned marketing subsidiary. This seemed to be successful in France.

United States

In implementing its new direct marketing approach in the U.S marker, BMW faced two alternatives. It could either take-over its present U.S. importer-distributor or establish a new and separate BMW marketing subsidiary as in France. The company wondered which of these alternatives would be best for the important U.S. market. BMW had about 250 dealers in the United States.

Problem

a) Do you see any disadvantage for BMW in going to direct distribution in foreign markets?

b) What advantages might the company realize by

operating through its own marketing subsidiaries?

c) In marketing the decision for the U.S. market, what questions would you ask? What variables would you consider?

SECTION FOUR

SHAGUN TYAGI

CASE - 1

A Ltd. Textile Manufacture Company

A Ltd. is textile manufacture company, struggling for its existence in competitive market. From past few years the company has been facing massive losses. Its top level managers decided to improve performance because only a well performed organization is able to satisfy the wants, needs and expectations of its stakeholders. Top level managers decided to adopt new technology for manufacturing to cope up with the rapidly changing business environment with an objective that in order to improve performance, an organization needs to continuously improve its effectiveness as well as efficiency.

A Ltd. has to organizations look to improve their market position for this they have to work more on creative and effective methods. Improving processes often means changing them or creating a new one altogether and technology can resist in making these improvements. Adopting technology with an objective to improve market position and overcoming from the problem of resistance to change.

For this organization generated huge amount of information which has become a major competitive factor in today's business world. There top level managers transformed this useful information into knowledge which they think leads to higher competitive advantage.

Providing the right persons with the information which is complete, correct, relevant and in-time is important to support strategic decision making for business. After implementation of such changes in organisation, many employees experienced cultural, financial, access and awareness barriers to learning. The global change is so rapid that employees in A Ltd. must continuously learn new skills at work rather than rely on the skills they bring with them. But however they resist the changes.

Problems

1. Do you think A Ltd. decision is correct to adopt new technology to gain the competitive advantage?
2. How will organisation deal with resistance to change? What are the barriers related to adoption of new technology?
3. Explain what techniques A Ltd should apply to overcome with resistance to change?

CASE - 2

Adoption of Internet Banking: ICICI bank as a case

A look at ICICI Bank

ICICI Bank is a multinational banking and financial

services company. ICICI Bank offers a wide range of financial products and services to corporate and retail customers. Analysts credit the bank's growth to a continuous focus on technological innovation. The driving factor for the rapid growth of ICICI Bank was its positioning as an innovative, technology-savvy, and customer-friendly bank. Realizing that they would need a robust core technology platform to help them achieve their business goals, management conducted an intense evaluation of several global vendors and ultimately selected the finale universal banking solution from Infosys (Infosys Technologies Ltd., 2009). An open systems approach and low total cost of ownership were among the key features of the system, which provided ebroking, call centre, online debit, consumer banking, corporate e-banking, credit cards, text message alerts, and mobile micro payment options.

Internet banking concept in India was initiated by ICICI bank in mild nineties as many new private sector banks came up with a new business model revolving around a strong information technology (IT) backbone. Though it started to facilitate information sharing, storing personal and financial information among banks. Recent development shows that most of brick and mortar banks have evolved themselves by shifting their focus towards rejuvenation and modernization of their own new ebanking capabilities. Internet banking services are progressively turning into a need with the introduction of mobile apps and Digital India initiative. This drastic change take place as we are moving towards a cashless society, where cash is replaced in electronic digital form. Digital methods of recording, managing, and exchanging money in commerce, investment is being experience by world wide.

Technological Innovations at ICICI Bank

Customer's dissatisfaction with traditional banking services and credit facilities has led to significant innovations in the banking industry. Given the fact that technology is a key enabler of process and product improvements, bank officials have come to realize the importance of incorporating the latest technological solutions into banking operations.

- For this ICICI Bank opened a broad network of Automated Teller Machines (ATMs) to make it easy for customers to withdraw funds. The early, ATMs were bank-specific, bank could not be used in another bank's ATMs.
- Another strategic move to sustain growth was to capture international business, especially that of non-resident Indians (NRIs) who utilized remittance services like internet banking.

Adopting Technology with an Eye Toward the Future

The increasingly competitive market for payment solutions and latest trends in banking were changing customers' responses to innovation and technology this meant that providers could not ignore the growing demand for user-friendly, single-integrated payment programs. Also, there was a strong need for lower development costs and shorter program implementation time. To meet the requirements of its end users, ICICI bank created a single integrated system for all stakeholders (ICICI Bank, 2016). This new system enabled the bank to keep float money within its system over longer periods of time, so end users would not have to wait to receive their payments. Even traditional customers were beginning to want simple and quick solutions for various services.

Problem

1. Does e-Banking provide a scope for banking institutions to expand their internet banking services to have a more sophisticated and wide customer base ?
2. The digital India initiative has created a new dimension for customers as well as the banks. Do such initiatives lead to enhanced trust in internet banking among customers or is just a hoax to create more business opportunities?

CASE - 3

Cartel formation between Vega Foodie and Banana Bakers

Vega Foodie and Banana Bakers are two big firms covering almost 60% share of food market selling their product with all other competitor. With a view to cope up with competition they come into an agreement to explicitly engage in fixing price to increase their market power. This agreement is popularly known as cartels.

Cartels usually formed in oligopoly market where there are a small number of sellers and usually sell homogeneous products.

An oligopoly is a market structure in which a few big firms dominate selling a similar product or we can say that when a market is shared between a few firms, it is said to be extremely concerted. Companies within oligopolies are competitors, but they tend to cooperate with each other in order to benefit as a whole, often leading to higher prices for consumers.

As per this formal agreement between Vega Foodie and Banana Bakers, both firms agreed to work together to determine jointly the level of output that each member will produce and/or the price that each member will charge. By working together, firms are able to behave like a monopolist this enable them to regulate supply in an effort to regulate or manipulate prices.

They successfully established a good relation with each other. But after some time it become difficult for them to maintain the cartels. The problem is that Banana Bakers tempted to cheat on their agreement to limit production. By producing more output than it has agreed to produce, it increases its share of the cartel's profits. Hence, there would no longer be any incentive for Vega Foodie to remain in the cartel.

Problems

1. How Vega Foodie and Banana Bakers will determine their level of output?

2. Is drawing demand curve is possible in case of oligopoly firm? If yes then how Vega Foodie and Banana Bakers will determine their demand curve?

CASE - 4

Acquisition of Companies for Long Term Survival - Case of Tata Steel and Corus

Keeping in mind, that the increase of inter-dependence of markets for various goods and services as well as increasing foreign competition, it is obvious, that today we live in a time of significant changes. That's why many companies are expanding their geographic reach and grow. Companies, which desire to grow, usually seek to take an

- additional market share, reach new customer base create economic profits
- Provide returns for their stakeholders, etc.
- As in case of Tata steel and Corus, they came into a agreement of acquisition to gain the following benefit.
- Increase market share
- Enhance product offerings and/or diversify product line
- Vertical integration of supply chain

- Gain access to patents, R&D or technology
- Potential tax benefits and shareholder value enhancement

Tata Steel is one of the biggest ever Indian's steel company and the Corus is Europe's second largest steel company. In 2007, Tata Steel and Corus plan an acquisition as a strategic choice for organisational growth and achievement of business goals including profit, empire building, market dominance, and long term survival. For this Tata Steel's takeover European steel major Corus for the price of $12.02 billion, making the

Indian company, the world's fifth-largest steel producer. Tata sponge iron was a steel producer provide steel at low cost and corus was also a steel producer sells high value product. The acquisition was intended to give Tata steel access to the European markets and to achieve potential synergies in the areas of manufacturing, procurement, R&D, logistics, and back office operations. Acquisition of these two firms represents the ultimate in change for a business.

Problems

1. Did the decision of Acquisition of Tata steel is correct. Comment?
2. According to you what steps should top level managers of this two company should follow for acquisition process?

CASE - 5

Product Positioning and Promotional Strategy of Glue Bond

Glue bond the on of the adhesive brand, enjoyed a leading position in the adhesive business in India with a maximum market share. According to some analysts, Glue bond's dominance in the Indian adhesive market could be attributed not only to the brand's inherent strength and quality but also to a series of advertising campaigns launched by the company over the years to promote the Glue bond brand. "Although Glue bond is not a consumer product, but it has managed to reach out to every Indian because of its brilliance and humour of the campaigns.

Glue bond is promoted as easy to use glue for carpenters, as an alternative to fat and collagen based adhesive which had to be boiled before application. Over the years, the brand had proved its mettle in terms of consistency, quality, and strong distribution method and customer relationship. It had become a generic name in the adhesive category in India. According to industry experts, Glue bond had strong brand equity and remained embedded in the minds and hearts of the customers. Since adhesive was a low involvement category, Glue bond adopted creative marketing strategies to increase the sales of the adhesive, they said. Over the years, Glue bond's simple, creative, and humorous advertisements clicked with customers and contributed to the success of the brand, opined industry experts.....

According to industry observers, Glue bond had managed to ensure a high recall value in the minds of consumers in spite of belonging to a largely B2B product category. Although Glue bond was a low involvement product, it had managed to reach out to every household in India due to the brilliance and humour behind its ad campaigns, said some industry observers. According to them, Glue bond had always used humour to reach out to the audience and had been successful in leaving a lasting impression on the minds of consumer through its hilarious ads. Its witty ads played an important role in making Glue bond a household name with tremendous brand recall. The ads were so successful that they managed to make an adhesive product like Glue bond into an FMCG item.

According to analysts, Glue bond's sustainable brand success was due to continuous innovation and the introduction of new and effective products across segments. With the introduction of new small-sized SKUs (Stock Keeping Units), deepening of the distribution network, and a series of brilliant advertisements, the company was able to create a pull for its brand that led to a strong increase in its sales.

Problems

1. Do Glue bond's attributes support their positioning statements?
2. Assess the competition. How are competitor products positioned?

CASE - 6

Dividend Policy for Modern Tech Ltd.

Modern Tech Ltd. is one of the leading information technology outsourcing services providers in India. The company provides business consultancy and outsourcing services to its clients all over India. Over the past five years the company has been paying dividends at high rate to its shareholders. However, this year, although the earnings of the company are high, its liquidity position is not so good. Thus, a firm's board of directors actually has made a specific distribution decision every time before dividend is declared because once the board declares a dividend; the corporation is legally obligated to make the payments. Therefore, top level managers thinking that dividend should not be declared unless a corporation is in a financial position to make the payment.

Moreover, the company plans to undertake new ventures in order to expand its business as it receive a wide variety of outsourcing work from other countries for computer or Internet related work, such as programming. Reason behind this is successful business expansion can put the firm in a positive place when it comes to acquiring necessary financing. This financing can be a lifeline to the business during the expansion process and a fallback after the expansion has occurred.

Company with increased market share and a solid financial position can get loan easily. Now there is an issue in for top level mangers to make a decision between retained earning or declaration of dividend. Because in case if they distribute dividend less than the expected dividend they may loss their shareholders and on other hand if they distribute maximum portion of earning as dividend their plan for expansion may effect.

Problems

1. Give any three reasons because of which you think Modern Tech Ltd. has been paying dividends at high rate to its shareholders over the past five years.
2. Comment upon the likely dividend policy of the company this years by stating any two reasons in support of your answer.

CASE - 7

Application of MM-Model in Shiva Corporation

Shiva Corporation is one of the fastest growing company selling electronic items like T.V, Fridge, AC etc. having 56% market share. But instead of this huge success company is criticized by many of its shareholders because they are not getting divided upto their expectation.

The Board of Directors (Board) of Indian consumer durable company the Shiva Corporation had not paid any dividend since it went public in the early 2000s. In the year 2015-16, this issue is handled by Institutional Investors Advisory Services organization, an advisory of financial market participants and they pointed out that Shiva Corporation had not paid dividends and alleged that it was utilizing the cash for other purposes.

The Board was of the opinion that its retention policy was in line with shareholders' interests and expectations. Also, in the policy document submitted on dividend distribution in compliance with the "Listing Regulations" notified by SEBI (Securities and Exchange Board of India, the regulator for the securities market in India), the Board clearly specified that its first priority was to utilize the profits to meet the capital expenditure requirements and to earmark the cash to meet potential in organic growth opportunities. This is the reason why they retain maximum portion of the earning and distributed only a small portion as dividend.

Problem

1. Apply hypothesis MM Model-to a Shiva Corporation.
2. Analyze Shiva Corporation's Dividend Policy using MM-hypothesis.

CASE - 8

Capital Structure of 'Krmaditya'

'Krmaditya' is a company enjoying market leadership in the textile brands segment. It renowned for its unique designs on Sarees and suits. Its portfolio includes two categories in the textile business namely **Cotton** and **Silk**.

'Krmaditya' become a brand for women's wearing Sarees and Suits, their speciality is that they are manufacturing their product in two fabric only and their unique designs on Suits and Sarees providing them a different identity in market. Their products are not only demanded in domestic country but they are getting demand from different countries too. Keeping in mind the growing demand for their product, they now plans to install new machines so that they can able to manufacture more units in given time.

Therefore, the company has planned to undertake investments of nearly Rs. 10 cores for its new line of business. They have number of financing option like debt financing, they can issue new shares or they also can borrow loan from other financial institutes.

Now top level managers of the company planning a capital structure for the firm and as per the current financial report, the interest coverage ratio of the company and return on investment is higher. Moreover, the corporate tax rate is high.

Problems

1. As a financial manager of the company, which source of finance will you opt for debt or equity, to raise the required amount of capital? Explain by giving any two suitable reasons in support of your answer.
2. Why the shareholder's of the company like to gain from the issue of debt by the company?

SECTION FIVE

AUTHOR VIVEK AGRAWAL

CASE - 1

Establishing a Luxury Brand in a Price-sensitive Market Like India: A Case of I-Phone

Once again Indian economy is expected to grow at large pace in the world, thus a major opportunity, especially since the China continues to show signs of slowdown. But Indian market is quiet different from any developed or emerging market and poses several challenges for foreign suppliers. One of them is the price-sensitive nature of Indian consumer which restricts the large manufacturers only to small portion of high-end consumers foregoing the real opportunity lies beyond this. This was applicable few years ago for Apple also and Indian consumers show no madness which was associated with its launches in many countries.

But, slowly Apple has started making inroads and India too becoming crazy over the new launches. In just last three-four years Indian markets are become lucrative for Apple's global business. i Phone have become part of primary class segment in Indian market. Along with car, smart phone has become a biggest status symbol for Indian consumers, and i Phone excels in that role.

As per the studies there is increase in per capita income with high economic growth, which results in shifting of consumption patterns from necessity items to optional consumption. Number of rich and middle income consumers has increased, with a subsequent reduction in the number of people below the poverty line. This results in growth of large aspirational class of peoples those who are not-so-rich but have significant disposable income and can experiment with brands. For this aspirational class which is growing by the day one of the attractive features of iPhone's is its out-of-reach pricing.

Another reason is consumer habit of Indian consumer that they will not buy when offered a basic product at $100 and advanced feature versions at $120 and $150 in fact here you have to market your product at $150 first, and then offer without additional features at $120 and basic product at $100. Lot of companies have already changed their approaches accordingly keeping the value of product same but giving importance to consumer habits. And even when following such an approach, it is important that the companies strive to keep the prices as low as possible. Incidentally, the Indian government's "Make in India" scheme, to encourage manufacturing within the country, will help foreign companies achieve just that.

Apple has also recognised this and had taken many initiatives like offering discounts, buybacks and EMI schemes. It also introduced a new 'Assembled in India' low priced iPhone SE. According to an estimate by Counterpoint Technology Market Research Apple had recorded 56% increase in shipping of iPhones in India from October 2015 to September 2016. In quarter ended March 2017, in contrast to slump in iPhone sales globally there is more than 20% growth in Apple's revenue in India.

Problems

1. What would be your suggestions for Promotional strategy for Apple in India? Is offering discounts and low priced phone can affects status symbol position of iPhone?
2. "India's growing aspirational class holds a lot of potential for Apple, which has just a 3% market share in India's smartphone market" Comment.

CASE - 2

Indian Family Business: Challenges for Success

Family businesses constitute most businesses in India. Economic liberalization and rapid expansion in the industrial base in recent years have not only created growth opportunities for many but also have tested their resource capabilities to respond to them. Multiple generations of a family are associated with the firm through leadership or ownership and influenced decision making. Some of the world's largest family-run businesses are Walmart (United States), Samsung Group (Korea), Tata Group (India) and Foxconn (Taiwan).

The high exposure to capital-intensive ventures in the metal, power and infrastructure sectors creates a stress for many family-owned businesses due to high debt and poor financial performance in these areas. This raises a few questions about the future of family enterprise in India. A case in point is the dissimilarity in the performance of the AV Birla Group and other branches of the family. Similarly, 1980s champions such as Nanda of Escorts, Modi and Bangur lost out in the 1990s due to the division of the original empires and resultant inability of individual branches to fund growth and expansion. Recent is the Tata group vs Cyrus Mistry exposing the power struggle between founders and professionals.

Experts feel that family-owned businesses will gradually lose their importance as capital availability improves and market institutions mature in India. They still see a future for family-owned businesses but only for those who focus on their core competencies and are global leaders. There is little hope for groups that are large but not industry leaders.

According to PwC India Family Business Survey 2016 Need for innovation is considered as a key challenge in the next 5 years by top executives of 56% Indian family businesses and 84% Indian family businesses are expected to grow either steadily or quickly and aggressively over the next 5 years. But only 15% of family businesses have a well defined, properly documented and communicated succession plan. 35% plan to pass on management to the next generation; whereas 48% plan to pass on ownership but bring in professionals for management.

In order to successfully balance the differing interests of one or more family members on the one hand and the interests of the business on the other hand people involved must show great competencies, character and commitment to do this work.

Problems

1. "Family-owned businesses will gradually lose their importance as capital availability improves and market institutions mature in India." Do you agree? Discuss by giving example of an Indian business.
2. Describe challenges for the success of family business in India.

CASE - 3

Modes of Motivation

Ravi, a shop floor manager, is a hardworking employee of Prakash steel company. He belongs to hardworking family. His needs for achievement and power were developed while he was growing up. He has been in his current position for the last ten years and the fact that he has not been promoted is great concern for him. In early days of life pay is enough to meet the needs. He is active outside the office especially with hobbies and recreational activities. In company he always had seen helping others in their works. But soon family demands starts rising and with current pay he is not able to sustain it. He becomes depressed and to make quick money he start gambling and generally spends a lot of money on it. All this start affecting his work and he often excuse him from performing important duties. For five years, his performance on the job was observed by his manager Mr. Sen., and he wanted to assign new project work that had come into their department to Ravi involving sufficient monetary reward also. And he was certain about his effectiveness in carrying out the task, once he commits himself to it, but current condition of Ravi making him doubtful.

Problems

1. By referring to various motivational models, suggest the needs seem to be most important for Ravi.
2. Is a monetary incentive enough to solve the problem? If not, suggest alternative solutions to be followed by Mr. Sen.

CASE - 4

Promotional Strategy for Khoobsurat

Khoobsurat is a regional skincare centre chain based in NCR. They have effectively used social media to grow their audience. In service industry, it's important to create credibility and present yourself favourably so as to increase revisits. Khoobsurat takes advantage of photos on Twitter and videos on Facebook or Whatsup groups to do this.

Khoobsurat regularly publish coupons, promote causes and share tips for their consumers or about important skin problems on twitter, facebook, whatsup and other social media.

Some advantages of creating a Whatsup or Facebook group:

- You can contact audience directly, with a high open rate.
- Social media provides robust statistics and moderation tools-HINT: make sure to create clear group guidelines.

Problems

1. Suggest suitable online promotional strategy for Khoobsurat to increase its clientele.
2. Discuss advantages and disadvantages of using online media vs traditional media.

CASE - 5

The Sachet Revolution

In June 2010, C.K. Ranganathan, 50, founder of CavinKare, had reasons to feel satisfied. In business circles, CavinKare is a legend - the David of the fast moving consumer goods, or FMCG, sector, which successfully took on Goliaths like HUL, and P&G. CavinKare's first and most memorable innovation, in 1983, was the sachet: it sold shampoo in tiny, low-priced sachets at a time when the big players only marketed it in high-priced bottles. By doing so it discovered a vast, untapped market and forced its big rivals to follow suit. Today 75-80 per cent of shampoos sold in India are in sachets, of which CavinKare has a 30 per cent share. Yet Ranganathan was worried. He was concerned that around seven of every 10 innovations presented to him were aimed at the relatively low-end segment of consumers. No doubt it was this segment that brought CavinKare its initial success, and still provided about 60 per cent of the company's revenues, but Ranganathan wanted to target the premium segments, where margins were much higher. He also felt that CavinKare had no longer a proactive organisation and his people were not learning enough.

"Innovation is important but without the right culture, it cannot be sustained."

Ranganathan in December 2010 come up with definite solution about how he wanted CavinKare to change. His first task was to get the employees to become more achievement oriented. He introduced a new working system for better and faster product development, shifted CavinKare's marketing office from Chennai to Mumbai and began looking around for acquisitions and tie-ups to bring premium products under his company's umbrella. The workforce was divided into creators who are associated with research and development, marketing and sales, enhancers associated with production, purchase, logistics and supply chain and protectors comprises accounts, finance and management information system team. Creators are the key group and were asked to come up with innovations that targeted the high end of the market.

Company want that 60 per cent of revenues to come from the premium segment. Ranganathan also got the team to start anticipating the competition's moves and prepare to counter them early. This helped when; rival Pantene slashed its shampoo sachet price from Rs 1.50 to Rs 1 to match CavinKare's Chik. It had the response a better formulation of shampoo - ready and launched it in less than a month. It was an improved product at the same price. CavinKare has also embraced the 'Blue Ocean Strategy' to identify uncontested market spaces and create products to fill them. For instance, it launched Indica 10, a hair dye which can be washed off within 10 minutes of applying it. Rival hair dye brands require at least 30 to 45 minutes to take effect.

Ranganathan's reforms have already started yielding results. The product development time has shrunk to 11 months from 12 months earlier. CavinKare is also making a conscious effort to reach all over Indian market. Pursuing Ranganathan's new thrust towards tie-ups, as well as towards improving premium market presence, the company has entered into a strategic alliance with Coty Inc. - the world's largest fragrance company. Today Cavinkare has 66% new product development success ratio compared to <5% industry norm. It transformed from a pure Personal Care player to a FMCG conglomerate with expertise in Dairy, Snacks, Food, Beverages and Professional Care business and has single R&D centre focuses on development of differentiated, innovative and proprietary products for all businesses.

Problems

1. Can the introduction of sachets by CavinKare be classified as a disruptive innovation in the shampoo market? Why or Why not?
2. Discuss the areas where Mr. Ranganathan focused to develop an innovative culture at CavinKare.

CASE - 6

Marketing and Distribution of Organic Aggs

Ravi and Chirag are two enterprising youth. They have passed out from IIM, Ahmedabad. They thought instead of doing a job, they will launch organic foods in Indian markets. Having learnt of the future conventional foods, they decided to venture into production and supply of organic eggs. Organic eggs are known to be craze among young health conscious young generation. For Ravi and Chirag fund raising was a serious handicap for mass production. However, the first trial batch of organic eggs that they produced was bought by local retail chain in Delhi. Further, the retail chain placed orders for supply of 125 dozens every week. Till now, small entrepreneurs had significant share in organic foods industry. Large companies have cold storage facilities and were more interested in the export market of organic vegetables.

Ravi and Chirag have set their sights high. They aim to sell organic foods in a very big way all over India and want to introduce organic vegetables. Organic vegetables have a great market potential and is a perishable food.

Problems

1. How will you advise Ravi and Chirag, as how to increase the consumer awareness about this new food?
2. What would be your suggestions for distribution channel for Organic vegetables?

CASE - 7

Struggling Period of Nestle-Winning Ways for Maggi

Since three decades Nestlé made a dedicated effort to build a beloved noodle brand Maggi in India. Then the world's biggest food and beverage company had to suffer a public relations debacle that cost it half a billion dollars.

It was a cautionary tale of mangled crisis management. On June 5, 2015, India's central food regulator authority FSSAI declared Maggi "unsafe and hazardous for human consumption" and announced a temporary ban on the manufacture, sale, and distribution of Maggi noodles. Because according reports of 30 government lab tests Nestlé's noodles contained excess amounts of lead. Nestlé lost at least $277 million in missed sales.

Another $70 million was spent to execute one of the largest food recalls in history. It is estimated that it also cause $200 million damage to its brand value. Why this happens, during one of his raid food inspector of Kanpur found that packets of Maggi do not have "no added MSG label" on them. And later on after a laboratory test Maggi sample had tested positive for MSG, or monosodium glutamate, a controversial ingredient that's legal in India but requires disclosure and a warning that the product is not recommended for children under 12 months old. As a flavour enhancer MSG is often associated with Chinese foods but since long time it has been blamed for everything from bad dreams to cancer-all claims that research has failed to validate.

The fact that the Maggi sample contained MSG when its packaging said it didn't was a violation punishable with a fine of up to 300,000 rupees-or about $4,500. Nestlé could have closed this matter there only by paying the penalty. But when Nestlé India was notified, the company denied adding MSG and appealed the finding. As a result, in June 2014, a second Maggi sample was sent to a different government laboratory in Kolkata. Nearly a year later, in April 2015, the results shows "MSG: Present." But surprisingly this reports also shows "Lead: 17.2 ppm." According to the report, the Maggi sample contained more than seven times the permissible level of lead-over 1,000 times more than the company claimed was in the product.

Following day the news come in a local newspaper followed by television media but Nestle does not respond. The Nestlé way is to deal with authorities directly rather than through the press. Nestlé India officials also say they were still collecting facts and performing self testing as much as possible. But what's the use of data if you don't explain yourself? To outsiders, too, Nestlé appeared paralyzed-or worse, guilty. Many Indians took the company's silence as a sign of wrongdoing.

Nearly a year after the ban following the court order, Maggi noodles are back, but somewhat riskily so. The product's future depends on two legal cases that are working their way through the Indian court system. Both pit Nestlé against the Indian government. Despite Nestlé's long history in India, the company's officials misread a fast-moving situation at every point. "This is a case where you can be so right and yet so wrong," says Nestlé CEO Paul Bulcke. "We had proper facts but not able to argue it proper. It's not a matter of being right. It's a matter of engaging the right way and finding a solution." He adds: "We live in an ambiguous world. We have to be able to cope with that."

Problems

1. What are the mistakes Nestle made in this crisis?
2. "This is a case where you can be so right and yet so wrong," says Nestlé CEO Paul Bulcke. Explain the statement and suggest the possible way to solution if you were the Country Head of India unit.

CASE - 8

Chemco Case

Started in 1980, Krishna Rubbers is a leading manufacturer of cycle and rickshaw tyres in the Indian and surrounding market. Since then, it has been under the charge of Mr. Krishna, the founder-owner of the firm. In 2009, the company decided to go for a diversification by expanding the product line. The new product was tyres for scooters. At the same time, Mr. Parekh was appointed the Senior Vice President of marketing in the company. But, sales in scooter tyres segment start dropping steadily. Mr. Parekh wanted to introduce some radical changes in the advertising and branding of the new business but the proposal was turned down by the old-fashioned Mr. Krishna.

At this juncture in 2012, the firm is losing heavily in the scooter tyre business as pollution norms banned 3 stroke scooters and as petrol prices are raising consumers are preferring high mileage motorcycles and company's market share of cycle and rickshaw tyres is also on a decline. Low priced tyres from China and increasing cost of raw materials also a major threat. Mr. Krishna has asked Mr. Parekh to show a turnaround in the company within a year.

Problems

1. Do SWOT analysis of the Krishna Rubbers.
2. What steps should Mr. Parekh take to bring the company out of its troubles?

CASE - 8

Chemco Case

Started in 1980, Krishna Rubbers is a leading manufacturer of cycle and rickshaw tyres in the Indian and surrounding market. Since then, it has been under the charge of Mr. Krishna, the founder-owner of the firm. In 2009, the company decided to go for a diversification by expanding the product line. The new product was tyres for scooters. At the same time, Mr. Parekh was appointed the Senior Vice President of marketing in the company. But, sales in scooter tyres segment start dropping steadily. Mr. Parekh wanted to introduce some radical changes in the advertising and branding of the new business but the proposal was turned down by the old-fashioned Mr. Krishna.

At this juncture in 2012, the firm is losing heavily in the scooter tyre business as pollution norms banned 3 stroke scooters and as petrol prices are raising consumers are preferring high mileage motorcycles and company's market share of cycle and rickshaw tyres is also on a decline. Low priced tyres from China and increasing cost of raw materials also a major threat. Mr. Krishna has asked Mr. Parekh to show a turnaround in the company within a year.

Problems

1. Do SWOT analysis of the Krishna Rubbers.
2. What steps should Mr. Parekh take to bring the company out of its troubles?